"Men must be governed by God or they will be ruled by tyrants". — **William Penn**

It's the duty of jurors, sheriffs, bailiffs and justices to resist all infringements upon the rights of the people without delay.

Thomas Jefferson said: *"Whenever people are well-informed they can be trusted with their own government"*.

Clearly the government cannot be in charge of deciding for themselves whether or not they should indict themselves on criminal charges or not. This is precisely why we have so much corruption in our government. It is the duty of the people to stand up as faithful and wise stewards (Luke 12:42) and bring the servants who think themselves as Master back into subjection.

COMMON LAW IS COMMON SENSE the question each jurist must ask himself is, "Is there an injured party"? There is a Common Law principle which states that for there to be a crime, there must *first* be a victim (*corpus delecti*); the state cannot be the injured party. In the absence of a victim there can be no crime. This is what the grand jurist must discover.

"The constitutions of most of our states assert that all power is inherent in the people; that they may exercise it by themselves in all cases to which they think themselves competent (as in electing their functionaries, executive and legislative, and deciding by a jury of themselves, both fact and law, in all judiciary cases in which any fact is involved) or they may ask by representatives, freely and equally chosen; that it is their right and duty to be at all times armed; to freedom of person; freedom of religion; freedom of property; and freedom of the press."
— [**Thomas Jefferson, letter to John Cartwright; June 5, 1824; "The Thomas Jefferson Papers," Library of Congress**]

1

GRAND JURORS – [25] It is the "DUTY" of the Common Law Grand Jury to expose all fraud and corruption, whether it is in the political or judicial realm, and stop it! The Authority of the Grand Jury is found only in the Bill of Rights, therefore it comes from God and not government - **Amendment V** – *"No person shall be held to answer for a capital, or otherwise infamous crime, unless on a presentment or indictment of a Grand Jury...".* It is in effect a fourth branch of government, "governed" and administered to directly by and on behalf of the American people.

TRIAL JURORS – [12] It is the duty of the Jury to execute Justice, and sometimes Mercy; their decisions cannot be second guessed. *"...the jury shall have the right to determine the law and the fact".* **New York Constitution Article 1. §8** *"As understood at common law and as used in constitutional provision, 'jury' imports a body of twelve men."* [**State v. Dalton, 206 N.C. 507, 174 S.E. 422, 424; People exrel. Cooley v. Wilder, 255 N.Y.S. 218, 222, 234 App. Div. 256; Hall v. Brown, 129 Kan. 859, 284 P. 396.**]

JURY NULLIFICATION *"The jury has a unalienable right to judge both the law as well as the fact in controversy."* **John Jay, 1st Chief Justice United States supreme Court, 1789.** *"The jury has the right to determine both the law and the facts."* **Samuel Chase, U.S. supreme Court Justice 1796, Signer of the unanimous Declaration** *"the jury has the power to bring a verdict in the teeth of both law and fact."* **Oliver Wendell Holmes, U.S. supreme Court Justice, 1902.**

Central to the history of trial by jury is the right of jurors to vote "not guilty" if the law is unjust or unjustly applied. When jurors acquit a factually guilty defendant, we say that the jury "nullified" the law. The Founding Fathers believed that juries in criminal trials had a role to play as the "conscience of the community," and relied on juries' "nullifying" to hold the government to the principles of the Constitution. *"Trust in the jury is, after all, one of the cornerstones of our entire criminal jurisprudence, and if that trust is without foundation we must re-examine a great deal more than just the nullification doctrine."* **Judge David L. Bazelon** There may be no feature more distinctive of American legal culture than the criminal trial jury. Americans have a deep and stubborn devotion to the belief that the guilt or innocence of a person accused of crime can only be judged fairly by a *"jury of his peers."* This notion is a particularly American one, although it was inherited from English common law during the Colonial era.

KENTUCKY RESOLUTIONS – A series of resolutions drawn up by Jefferson, and adopted by the legislature of Kentucky in 1799, protesting against the "alien and sedition laws," declaring their illegality, announcing the strict constructionist theory of the federal government, and declaring "nullification" to be "the rightful remedy."

JUSTICE – It is the duty of the Justice to do justice. In common law, the title given in England to the judges of the king's bench and the common pleas, and in America to the judges of the supreme court of the United States and of the appellate courts of many of the states. In the most extensive sense of the word "justice" differs little from "virtue"; for it includes within itself the whole circle of virtues. Yet the common distinction between them is that which, considered positively and in itself, is called "virtue," when considered relatively and with respect to others has the name of "justice," being in itself a part of "virtue," is confined to things simply good or evil, and consists in a man's taking such a proportion of them as he ought. **[Bouvier]**

THE SOURCE OF VIRTUE is found in **Luke 6:19**. *"And the whole multitude sought to touch him: for there went virtue out of him, and healed them all."* Therefore a Justice is to reflect divine qualities, as we read in **Phil 4:8**. *"Finally, brethren, whatsoever things are true, whatsoever things are honest, whatsoever things are just, whatsoever things are pure, whatsoever things are lovely, whatsoever things are of good report; if there be any virtue, and if there be any praise, think on these things."*

SHERIFF - *"America will never be destroyed from the outside. If we falter and loose our freedoms, it will be because we destroyed ourselves."* - **Abraham Lincoln**. The county Sheriff is the last line of defense when it comes to upholding and defending the Constitution. The Sheriff's duties and obligations go far beyond writing tickets, arresting criminals and operating jails. The Sheriff also has an obligation to protect the Constitutional rights of the citizens in our counties. This includes the right to free speech, the right to assemble, and the right to bear arms. Remember the oath.

Sheriffs took an oath to uphold and defend the Constitution, from enemies foreign AND domestic. In the history of our world, it is government tyranny that has violated the freedoms granted to us by our Creator more than any other. And it is the duty of the Sheriff to protect his county from those who would take away our freedoms, both foreign AND domestic – whether it is a terrorist from Yemen or a bureaucrat from Washington, DC.

BAILIFF - Officers who perform the duties of sheriffs within liberty or privileged jurisdictions in which formerly the King's writ could not be executed by the sheriff. One to whom some authority, care, guardianship, or jurisdiction is delivered, committed, or entrusted; one who is deputed or appointed to take charge of another's affairs; an overseer or superintendent; a keeper, protector, or guardian; a steward. Spelman. A sheriff's officer or deputy. **1 Bl. Comm. 344.** A court attendant.

It is the duty of all of the above to correct injustice in as much as it is in their power to do so. If correction is not possible it is the duty of the court officer(s) to report the problem to the protectors of the People, the Grand Jury, in who's' hand justice has been entrusted.

I. US. CODES
Remedy of the people when rights are violated.

USC 18 §2382 - Misprision of treason: Whoever having knowledge of treason, conceals and does not make known the same to some judge is guilty of treason for contempt against the sovereign and shall be fined under this title or imprisoned not more than seven years, or both.

USC 18 §201 - BRIBERY: If any public official directly or indirectly gives, offers, or promises anything of value to any person to influence any official act.

USC 18 §241 - CONSPIRACY AGAINST RIGHTS: If two or more persons conspire to injure, oppress, threaten, or intimidate any person in any State in the free exercise or enjoyment of any right they shall be fined under this title or imprisoned not more than ten years, or both.

USC 18 §242 - DEPRIVATION OF RIGHTS UNDER COLOR OF LAW: Whoever, under color of any law, statute, ordinance, regulation, or custom, willfully subjects any person in any State to the deprivation of any rights shall be fined under this title or imprisoned not more than one year, or both.

USC 18 §2071 - Concealment, etc.: Whoever willfully and unlawfully conceals, removes, mutilates, obliterates, or destroys, or attempts to do so, documents filed or deposited with any clerk or officer of any court, shall be fined or imprisoned not more than three years, or both.

USC 18 §2076 - CLERK IS TO FILE: Whoever, being a clerk willfully refuses or neglects to make or forward any report, certificate, statement, or document as required by law, shall be fined under this title or imprisoned not more than one year, or both.

USC 42 §1983 - CIVIL ACTION FOR DEPRIVATION OF RIGHTS: Every person who, under color of any statute, ordinance, regulation, custom, or usage, of any State subjects, or causes to be subjected, any person within the jurisdiction thereof to the deprivation of any rights, privileges, or immunities secured by the Constitution and laws, shall be liable to the party injured in an action at law.

USC 42 1985 - CONSPIRACY TO INTERFERE WITH CIVIL RIGHTS: If two or more persons in any State or Territory conspire for the purpose of depriving, either directly or indirectly, any person's rights the party so injured or deprived may have an action for the recovery of damages against any one or more of the conspirators.

USC 42 §1986 - ACTION FOR NEGLECT TO PREVENT: Every person who, having knowledge that any of the wrongs conspired to be done or are about to be committed, and having power to prevent or aid in preventing the commission of the same, neglects or refuses so to do, if such wrongful act be committed, shall be liable to the party injured.

II. ALL IS MINE

Job 41:11 *"Whatsoever is under the whole heaven is mine."*; **Ezek 18:4** *"Behold, all souls are mine; as the soul of the father, so also the soul of the son is mine."*; **Exo 19** *"Now therefore, if ye will obey my voice indeed, and keep my covenant, then ye shall be a peculiar treasure unto me above all people: for all the earth is mine"*; **Psa 50:12** *"If I were hungry, I would not tell thee: for the world is mine, and the fullness thereof."*; **Prov 8:14** *"Counsel is mine, and sound wisdom: I am understanding; I have strength."*

III. GOVERNMENT BY CONSENT

Our founders purposely placed the power of the Grand Jury in the "Bill of Rights" to make it clear that it belongs to the people and the government is not to violate it. It is the "ultimate power" of the people which allows them to consent or not to the actions of their servant government. It also prevents government from unrighteous prosecutions by forcing the government to seek permission from the people before criminal charges can be filed, if the people refuse, it cannot go forward. By understanding this principle it becomes clear that the government has no authority to control your behavior and therefore neither do legislators without your consent.

The **Declaration of Independence** says: *"We hold these truths to be self-evident, that all men are created equal, that they are endowed by their Creator with certain unalienable Rights, that among these are Life, Liberty and the pursuit of Happiness. -- That to secure these rights, Governments are instituted among Men, __deriving their just powers from the consent of the governed__".*

ALL MEN DECIDE FOR THEMSELVES whether they want to participate in the institutions of men or not. The United States Supreme Court confirmed this when they said: "...every man is independent of all laws, except those prescribed by nature. He is not bound by any institutions formed by his fellowman without his consent." [**Cruden v. Neale, 2 N.C. 338 May Term 1796.**]

IV. ONLY PEOPLE CAN FILE
A CRIMINAL COMPLAINT

There are only *three ways* a court can hear a criminal complaint: **(1)** One or more of the people sign a sworn affidavit that they have been injured; **(2)** A prosecutor, on behalf of the government brings an accusation before the Grand Jury and the Grand Jury either indicts or does nothing; **(3)** The Grand Jury by its "own will" can investigate merely on suspicion that the law is being violated, or even because it wants assurance that it is not, and if it finds wrong-doing it can present it to the court and it must go to trial. No one can second guess the Grand Jury, unless the Grand Jury's action violates another's unalienable rights.

PRINCIPLE OF LIBERTY - Consent and Jurisdiction; it's all about Consent and Jurisdiction. In order to possess liberty it is extremely important that you understand Consent; our servant government cannot do anything without your consent.

CONSENT OF AUTHORITY - We read in the Declaration of Independence, *"We hold these truths to be self-evident, that all men are created equal, that they are endowed by their Creator with certain unalienable Rights, that among these are Life,*

*Liberty and the pursuit of Happiness. That to secure these rights, Governments are instituted among Men, **deriving their just powers from the consent of the governed**."* Any authority our servants have is by our consent; if they act outside their authority they are subject to criminal charges under **US Codes 42 and 18** and liable for damages under US Codes and common law.

CONSENT TO INDICT - The Fifth Amendment states: "No person shall be held to answer for a capital, or otherwise infamous crime, unless on a presentment or indictment of a Grand Jury..." Therefore our servant government requires the people to get an indictment (grand jury). Judges (servants) have no authority to make a ruling or a judgment on people (masters) without your consent, in legal terms when the judge asks you *"do you understand"*, he means do you **"stand under"** the authority of his court, so when you say "yes", you give *him/her/the court* jurisdiction over you!

ONLY PEOPLE CAN JUDGE - Our US Constitution only authorizes "common law courts" a.k.a. "courts of record". A court of record removes the power of the Judge to make a ruling, his role is that of the "administrator" of the court. The final determinator is the "tribunal" who is either the "sovereign plaintiff" or a "jury". Remember the servant cannot rule over the master; can the clay rule over the potter?

"...every man is independent of all laws, except those prescribed by nature. He is not bound by any institutions formed by his fellowman without his consent." [**Cruden v. Neale**] Here is Liberty, if "YOU" do not give a court consent, they have no "JURISDICTION" over "YOU"!

Under US Codes 42 and 18 when you are detained, without your consent, for violating a statute, you have just been kidnapped and if the Judge sets a bail he just set a ransom and when the prosecutor confirms the charges he becomes part of a conspiracy and YOU can put the conspirators in jail and sue them for damages. It's all about Jurisdiction and Consent.

8

V. THE REAL LAW

"The common law is the real law, the Supreme Law of the land, the code, rules, regulations, policy and statutes are "not the law", [**Self v. Rhay, 61 Wn (2d) 261**] Legislated statutes enforced upon the people in the name of law are a fraud. They have no authority and are without mercy. Justice without mercy is Godless and therefore repugnant to our United States Constitution. Lawmakers were given authority by the people to legislate codes, rules, regulations, and statutes which are policies, procedures, and "law" <u>to control the behavior of bureaucrats, elected and appointed officials, municipalities and agencies</u>, but were never given authority to control the behavior of the people, as we read in a US Supreme court decision *"All codes, rules, and regulations are for government authorities only, not human/creators in accordance with God's laws. All codes, rules, and regulations are unconstitutional and lacking due process..."* [**Rodriques v. Ray Donavan (U.S. Department of Labor) 769 F. 2d 1344, 1348 (1985)**] and again *"All laws, rules and practices which are repugnant to the Constitution are null and void"* [**Marbury v. Madison, 5th US (2 Cranch) 137, 174, 176,(1803)**]

Legislators simply don't have the authority to <u>rule-make</u> *"Where rights secured by the Constitution are involved, there can be <u>no rule making</u> or legislation which would abrogate them"*. [**Miranda v. Arizona, 384 U.S. 436, 491**] God breaks down the law as follows: *"And Jesus answered him, The first of all the commandments is, Hear, O Israel; The Lord our God is one Lord: And thou shalt love the Lord thy God with all thy heart, and with all thy soul, and with all thy mind, and with all thy strength: this is the first commandment. And the second is like, namely this, Thou shalt love thy neighbour as thyself. There is none other commandment greater than these"*. [**Mark 12:29-31**] Although it is a sin, punishable only by the Judge of the Universe, to break the commandment to love, in your mind, words, and deeds, it does not become a crime, punishable by man, until your words and deeds are expressed in "actions" that injure another.

Thomas Jefferson said: *"I would rather be exposed to the inconveniences attending too much liberty than those attending too small a degree of it"*. If one of the people exercises his free will to carry a weapon, travel, practice law, park without depositing money in a meter, use hemp, pharmaceuticals, alcohol, vitamins, minerals or any other substance for medicinal or recreational purposes the legislators do not have the authority to impose a fine, license or make a right a crime.

VI. RIGHTS AND SOVEREIGNTY

Only people are sovereign and have rights; bureaucrats, in their capacity, are not sovereign and have no rights, they have authority given by the people and are subject to the statutes. *"The state cannot diminish rights of the people."* [**Hurtado v. People of the State of California, 110 U.S. 516**] *"The assertion of federal rights,* [Bill of Rights] *when plainly and reasonably made, is not to be defeated under the name of local practice"*. [**Davis v. Wechsler, 263 US 22, 24**] *"Where rights secured by the Constitution are involved, there can be no rule making or legislation which would abrogate them."* [***Miranda v. Arizona, 384 US 436, 491***] *"There can be no sanction or penalty imposed upon one because of this exercise of constitutional rights."* [**Sherer v. Cullen, 481 F 946**] *"Sovereignty itself is, of course, not subject to law, for it is the author and source of law;"* [**Yick Wo v. Hopkins, 118 US 356, 370 (Undersigned is Sovereign and no court has challenged that status/standing)**]

To deprive the People of their sovereignty it is first necessary to get the People to agree to submit to the authority of the entity they have created. That is done by getting them to claim they are citizens of that entity **(see Const. for the U.S.A., XIV Amendment, for the definition of a "citizen of the United States".)**

VII. LICENSING LIBERTY

"No state shall convert a liberty into a license, and charge a fee therefore." [**Murdock v. Pennsylvania, 319 U.S. 105**]

"If the State converts a right (liberty) into a privilege, the citizen can ignore the license and fee, and engage in the right (liberty) with impunity." [**Shuttlesworth v. City of Birmingham, Alabama, 373 U.S. 262**]

VIII. REMEDY FOR EVERY INJURY

William Blackstone - (a legal maxim) Every right when withheld must have a remedy, and every injury its proper redress. In the third volume of his Commentaries, page 23, Blackstone states two cases in which a remedy is afforded by mere operation of law. *"In all other cases,* he says, *it is a general and indisputable rule that where there is a **legal right**, there is also a **legal remedy** by suit or action at law whenever that right is invaded."* And afterwards, page 109 of the same volume, he says, *"I am next to consider such injuries as are cognizable by the Courts of common law. And herein I shall for the present only remark that all possible injuries whatsoever that did not fall within the exclusive cognizance of either the ecclesiastical, military, or maritime tribunals are, for that very reason, within the cognizance of the common law courts of justice, for it is a settled and invariable principle in the laws of England that every right, when withheld, must have a remedy, and every injury its proper redress."* [**5 U.S. 137, Marbury v. Madison**] *"The Government of the United States has been emphatically termed a government of laws, and not of men. It will certainly cease to deserve this high appellation if the laws furnish no remedy for the violation of a vested legal right."* [**Marbury v. Madison, 5 U.S. 137 (1803)**]

"...that statutes which would deprive a citizen of the rights of person or property without a regular trial, according to the course and usage of common law, would not be the law of the land." [**Hoke vs. Henderson,15, N.C.15,25 AM Dec 677**].

"...the right to be let alone is the most comprehensive of rights and the right most valued by civilized men. To protect that right, every <u>unjustifiable intrusion</u> by the government upon the

11

privacy of the individual, whatever the means employed, must be deemed a violation of the Fourth Amendment." [**Olmstead v. U.S., 277 U.S. 438, 478 (1928)**].

IX. COURT

The court belongs to the sovereign plaintiff (people). Black's Law Dictionary, 5th Edition, page 318 defines the ***court*** as *"The person and suit of the sovereign; the place where the sovereign sojourns with his regal retinue, wherever that may be."*

In the US Supreme Court case *Isbill v. Stovall* the court is defined as *"An agency of the sovereign created by him directly or indirectly under his authority, consisting of one or more officers, established and maintained for the purpose of hearing and determining issues of law and fact regarding legal rights and alleged violations thereof, and of applying the sanctions of the law, authorized to exercise its powers in the course of law at times and places previously determined by lawful authority."*

JUDICIAL NOTICE

"Judicial notice, or knowledge upon which a judge is bound to act without having it proved in evidence." **Black's Law 4th edition** Take Judicial notice of AMERICAN JURIS PRUDENCE BOOK 16: CONSTITUTION LAW SECTION which a judge is bound by oath to obey.

Judges Sworn To Obey Constitution Irrespective Of Opinion & Consequences — Constitution Rules Over Statutes

"Since the Constitution is intended for the observance of the judiciary as well as other departments of government, and the judges are sworn to support its provisions, the courts are not at liberty to overlook or disregard its commands or counteract evasions thereof, it is their duty in authorized proceedings to give full effect to the existing Constitution and to obey all

constitutional provisions irrespective of their opinion as to the wisdom or the desirability of such provisions and irrespective of the consequences, thus it is said that the courts should be in our alert to enforce the provisions of the United States Constitution <u>and guard against their infringement</u> by legislative fiat or otherwise in accordance with these basic principles, the rule is fixed that the duty in the proper case to declare a law unconstitutional cannot be declined and must be performed in accordance with the delivered judgment of the tribunal before which the validity of the enactment it is directly drawn into question. <u>If the Constitution prescribes one rule and the statute another in a different rule, it is the duty of the courts to declare that the Constitution and not the statute governs</u> in cases before them for judgment." [**16Am Jur 2d., Sec. 155:, emphasis added**]

SUPREMACY CLAUSE

"This Constitution, and the laws of the United States which shall be made in pursuance thereof; and all treaties made, or which shall be made, under the authority of the United States, shall be the supreme law of the land; and the judges in every state shall be bound thereby, anything in the Constitution or laws of any State to the contrary notwithstanding." [**US Constitution**]

"...Thus, the particular phraseology of the constitution of the United States confirms and strengthens the principle, supposed to be essential to all written constitutions, that <u>a law repugnant to the constitution is void</u>, and that courts, as well as other departments, are bound by that instrument." After more than 200 years this decision still stands. [**Marbury v. Madison 5 U.S. 137 (1803)**]

COMMON LAW IS STILL THE LAW OF THE LAND

All cases which have cited *Marbury v. Madison* to the Supreme Court have never been over turned. [**See Shephard's Citation of**

Marbury v. Madison]

The Constitution was ordained and established by the people "for" the United States of America a.k.a. government. Therefore government was created by an act of the people therefore the created cannot trump the creator. *"If any statement, within any law which is passed, is unconstitutional, the whole law is unconstitutional..."* [**Marbury v. Madison: 5 US 137 (1803)**] ...therefore no legislation.

"...statutes which would deprive a citizen of the rights of person or property without a regular trial, according to the course and usage of common law, would not be the law of the land." [**Hoke vs. Henderson,15, N.C.15,25 AM Dec 677**].

"Where rights secured by the Constitution are involved, there can be no rule making or legislation which would abrogate them." [**Miranda v. Arizona, 384 U.S. 436, 491**]

INTERPRETATION IN FAVOR OF THE PEOPLE

Any constitutional provision intended to confer a benefit should be liberally construed in favor in the clearly intended and expressly designated beneficiary. *"That a constitution should receive a literal interpretation in favor of the Citizen, is especially true, with respect to those provisions which were designed to safeguard the liberty and security of the Citizen in regard to person and property."* [**16Am Jur 2d: 16Am Jur 2d., Sec. 97; Bary v. United States - 273 US 128**]

NO EMERGENCY HAS JUST CAUSE TO SUPPRESS THE CONSTITUTION

"While an emergency can not create power, and no emergency justifies the violation of any of the provisions of the United States Constitution or States Constitutions, Public emergency, such as economic depression for especially liberal construction of constitutional powers, has been declared that because

14

of national emergency, it is the policy of the courts of times of national peril, so liberally to construe the special powers vested in the chief executive as to sustain and effectuate the purpose there of, and to that end also more liberally to construed the constituted division and classification of the powers of the co-ordinate branches of the government and in so far as may not be clearly inconsistent
with the constitution." [**16Am Jur 2d., Sec. 98**]

CONSTITUTIONS MUST BE CONSTRUED TO REFERENCE THE COMMON LAW — SUMMARY PROCEEDINGS ARE NULL & VOID

"As to the construction, with reference to Common Law, an important cannon of construction is that constitutions must be construed to reference the Common Law." "The Common Law, so permitted destruction of the abatement of nuisances by summary proceedings and it was never supposed that a constitutional provision was intended to interfere with this established principle and although there is no common law of the United States in a sense of a national customary law as distinguished from the common law of England, adopted in the several states. In interpreting the Federal Constitution, recourse may still be had to the aid of the Common Law of England. It has been said that without reference to the common law, the language of the Federal Constitution could not be understood." [**16Am Jur 2d., Sec. 114**]

SHALL NOT INFRINGE

"Various facts of circumstances extrinsic to the Constitution are often resorted to, by the courts, to aid them in determining its meaning, as previously noted, however such extrinsic aids may not be resorted to where the provision in the question is clear and unambiguous in such a case the courts must apply the terms of the Constitution as written and they are not at liberty to search for meanings beyond the instrument." [**16Am Jur 2d., Sec. 117**]

IRRECONCILABLE CONFLICT BETWEEN STATUTE AND CONSTITUTION IS TO BE RESOLVED IN FAVOR OF CONSTITUTIONALITY AND THE BENEFICIARY

"In all instances, where the court exercises its power to invalidate legislation on constitutional grounds, the conflict of the statute, with the constitution must be irreconcilable. Thus a statute is not to be declared unconstitutional unless so inconsistent with the constitution that it cannot be enforced without a violation thereof. A clear incompatibility between law and the Constitution must exist before the judiciary is justified holding the law unconstitutional. This principle is in line with the rule that doubts that the constitutionality should be resolved in favor of the constitutionality and the beneficiary." [**16Am Jur 2d., Sec. 255**]

SUPREME LAW IS THE BASES OF ALL LAW. ALL FICTION OF LAW IS NULL AND VOID

Nisi prius courts rely on statutes, which is fiction of law, that seeks to control the behavior of the sovereign people of New York and other states, who are under common law, not statutes, and who ordained and established the law, therefore legislators cannot legislate the behavior of the people.

"No provision of the Constitution is designed to be without effect," "Anything that is in conflict is null and void of law". "Clearly, for a secondary law to come in conflict with the supreme Law is illogical, for certainly, the supreme Law would prevail over all other laws and certainly our forefathers had intended that the supreme Law would be the basis of all law and for any law to come in conflict would be null and void of law, it would bare no power to enforce, it would bare no obligation to obey, it would purport to settle as if it had never existed, for unconstitutionality would date from the enactment of such a law, not from the date so branded in an open court of law, no courts are bound to uphold it, and no Citizens are bound to obey it. It operates as a near nullity or a fiction of law."

16

"All codes, rules, and regulations are for government authorities only, not human/creators in accordance with God's laws. All codes, rules, and regulations are unconstitutional and lacking due process..." [**Rodriques v. Ray Donavan**]

"The common law is the real law, the Supreme Law of the land, the code, rules, regulations, policy and statutes are not the law." [**Self v. Rhay, 61 Wn (2d) 261**]

NO ONE IS BOUND TO OBEY AN UNCONSTITUTIONAL LAW AND NO COURTS ARE BOUND TO ENFORCE IT

"The general rule is that a unconstitutional statute, whether Federal or State, though having the form and name of law is in reality no law, but is wholly void and ineffective for any purpose since <u>unconstitutionality dates from the enactment</u> and not merrily from the date of the decision so braining it. <u>An unconstitutional law in legal contemplation is as inoperative as if it never had been passed</u>. Such a statute lives a question that it purports to settle just as it would be had the statute <u>not ever</u> been enacted. No repeal of an enactment is necessary, since <u>an unconstitutional law is void</u>. The general principle follows that it imposes no duty, conveys no rights, creates no office, bestows no power of authority on anyone, affords no protection and justifies no acts performed under it. A contract which rests on an unconstitutional statute creates no obligation to be impaired by subsequent legislation. <u>No one is bound to obey an unconstitutional law</u>. <u>No courts are bound to enforce it</u>. Persons convicted and fined under a statute subsequently held unconstitutional may recover the fines paid. A void act cannot be legally inconsistent with a valid one and an unconstitutional law cannot operate to supersede an existing valid law. Indeed, in so far as a statute runs counter to the fundamental law of the land, it is superseded there by. Since an unconstitutional statute cannot repeal, or in anyway effect an existing one, if a repealing statute is unconstitutional, the statute which it attempts to repeal, remains in full force and effect and where a statute in which it attempts to repeal remains in

full force and effect and where a clause repealing a prior law is inserted in the act, which act is unconstitutional and void, the provision of the repeal of the prior law will usually fall with it and will not be permitted to operate as repealing such prior law. The general principle stated above applied to the constitution as well as the laws of the several states insofar as they are repugnant to the constitution and laws of the United States." [**16Am Jur 2d., Sec. 256**]

CONGRESS CANNOT ALTER RIGHTS

"On the other hand it is clear that Congress cannot by authorization or ratification <u>give the slightest effect to a state law</u> or constitution <u>which is in conflict with the Constitution of the United States.</u>" [**16Am Jur 2d., Sec. 258**]

RIGHTS DO NOT COME IN DEGREES

"Although it is manifested that an unconstitutional provision in the statute is not cured because included in the same act with valid provisions and that there are no degrees of constitutionality." [**16Am Jur 2d., Sec. 260**]

STATES CANNOT LICENSE RIGHTS

"A state may not impose a charge for the enjoyment of a right granted by the Federal Constitution and that a flat license tax here involves restraints in advance of the constitutional liberties of Press and Religion and inevitably tends to suppress their existence. That the ordinance is non-discriminatory and that it applies also to peddlers of wares and merchandise is immaterial. The liberties granted by the first amendment are in a preferred position. Since the privilege in question is guaranteed by the Federal Constitution and exists independently of the states authority, the inquiry as to whether the state has given something for which it cannot ask a return, is irrelevant. <u>No state may convert any secured liberty into a privilege and issue</u>

18

a license and a fee for it." [**Mudook v. Penn. 319 US 105:(1943)**]

"If the state does convert your right into a privilege and issues a license and a fee for it, <u>you can ignore the license and a fee and engage the right with impunity</u>." [**Shuttlesworth v. Birmingham AI. 373 US 262:(1962)**]

OFFICERS OF THE COURT HAVE NO IMMUNITY FROM LIABILITY WHEN VIOLATING CONSTITU-TIONAL RIGHTS

"The right of action created by statute relating to deprivation, under color of law, of a right secured by the Constitution and the laws of the United States, and some claims which are based solely on statutory violations of Federal Law and applied to the claim that claimants had been deprived of their rights, in some capacity, to which they were entitled." **Owen v. Independence 100 Vol. Supreme Court Reports 1398:(1982); Main v. Thiboutot 100 Vol. Supreme Court Reports. 2502:(1982)**

Title 18 US Code Sec. 241 & Sec. 242: *"<u>If upon conviction</u>, you are subject to a $10,000.00 fine, ten years in jail, or both, and <u>if theft results</u>, life in prison."* **Title 42 US Code Sec. 1983, Sec. 1985, & Sec. 1986**: <u>Clearly established the right to sue anyone who violates your constitutional rights</u>. The Constitution guarantees: he who would unlawfully jeopardize your property loses property to you, and that's what justice is all about. *"Judges are deemed to know the law and are sworn to uphold it and can hardly claim that they acted in good faith for willful deformation of a law and certainly <u>cannot plead ignorance of the law</u>, for that would make the law look unintelligent for a knowledgeable judge to claim ignorance of a law, when a Citizen on the street cannot claim ignorance of the law. <u>Therefore, there is no judicial immunity</u>."*

X. CONSTITUTIONAL PREAMBLES

Both Constitutions (US & NY, and the Constitution of any real Republic) the operative word is "establish" and ordain. The People existed in their own individual sovereignty before the Constitution was enabled. When the People "establish" a Constitution, there is nothing in the word "establish" that signifies that they have yielded any of their sovereignty to the agency they have created. To interpret otherwise would convert the Republic into a Democracy (Republic vs. Democracy).

XI. GOVERNMENT

We the people are a Republic, not a Democracy which is just the first step to an Oligarchy.

REPUBLICAN GOVERNMENT. One in which the powers of sovereignty are vested in the people and are exercised by the people, either directly, or through representatives chosen by the people, to whom those powers are specially delegated. **[In re Duncan, 139 U.S. 449, 11 S.Ct. 573, 35 L.Ed. 219; Minor v. Happersett, 88 U.S. (21 Wall.) 162, 22 L.Ed. 627. Black's Law Dictionary, Fifth Edition, p. 626]**

DEMOCRATIC GOVERNMENT. That form of government in which the sovereign power resides in and is exercised by the whole body of free citizens directly or indirectly through a system of representation, as distinguished from a monarchy, aristocracy, or oligarchy. **[Black's Law Dictionary, 5th Edition, p. 388; Bond v. U.S. SCOTUS] recognizes personal sovereignty, June 16, 2011]**

XII. DUTY OF COURTS

"It is the duty of the courts to be watchful for the Constitutional rights of the citizen and against any stealthy encroachments thereon". **[Boyd v. United States, 116 U.S. 616, 635]**
"It will be an evil day for American Liberty if the theory of a

government outside supreme law finds lodgment in our consti-tutional jurisprudence. No higher duty rests upon this Court than to exert its full authority to prevent all violations of the principles of the Constitution." **[Downs v. Bidwell, 182 U.S. 244 (1901)]** *"We (judges) have no more right to decline the exercise of jurisdiction which is given, than to usurp that which is not given. The one or the other would be treason to the Constitution."* **[Cohen v. Virginia, (1821), 6 Wheat. 264 and U.S. v. Will, 449 U.S. 200]** *"It may be that it is the obnoxious thing in its mildest form; but illegitimate and unconstitutional practices get their first footing in that way; namely, by silent approaches and slight deviations from legal modes of proce-dure. This can only be obviated by adhering to the rule that constitutional provisions for the security of persons and prop-erty should be liberally construed. A close and literal construc-tion deprives them of half their efficacy, and leads to gradual depreciation of the right, as if it consisted more in sound than in substance. <u>It is the duty of the Courts to be watchful for the Constitutional Rights of the Citizens</u>, and against any stealthy encroachments thereon. Their motto should be Obsta Principiis."* **[Boyd v. United, 116 U.S. 616 at 635 (1885)]**

XIII. COURTS OF RECORD ARE COMMON LAW COURTS AND THEREFORE COURTS OF JUSTICE

AT LAW. [Bouvier's Law, 1856 Edition] This phrase is used to point out that a thing is to be done according to the course of the common law; it is distinguished from a proceeding in equity.

Any court that ignores due process, all statutory courts ignore due process, is not a common law court, common law courts are "courts of record" in all courts of record the tribunal is the sovereign plaintiff(s) of the court or the Jury. The Justice is the administrator and reflects the wish of the sovereign, or jury, because <u>the people rule</u>, <u>not government servants</u>. The following "Law of the Land" proves this point.

This Constitution, and the laws of the United States which shall be made in pursuance thereof; and all treaties made, or which shall be made, under the authority of the United States, shall be the supreme **law of the land**; and the judges in every state shall be bound thereby, anything in the Constitution or laws of any State to the contrary notwithstanding. **[US Constitution, Art.6, clause 2]**

Law of the land, "due course of law" and "due process of law" are synonymous. **[People v. Skinner, Cal., 110 P.2d 41, 45; State v. Rossi, 71 R.I. 284, 43 A.2d 323, 326; Direct Plumbing Supply Co. v. City of Dayton, 138 Ohio St. 540, 38 N.E.2d 70, 72, 137 A.L.R. 1058; Stoner v. Higginson, 316 Pa. 481, 175 A. 527, 531]**

New York State Constitution Article VI. b. The court of appeals, the **supreme court** including the appellate divisions thereof, the court of claims, the county court, the surrogate's court, the family court, the courts or court of civil and criminal jurisdiction of the city of New York, and such other courts as the legislature may determine **shall be courts of record**. Courts are divided generally into courts of record and those that are not of record. A court of record is a judicial tribunal having attributes and exercising functions independently of the person designated generally to hold it, and **proceeding according to the course of the common law**.

In a court of record the acts and judicial proceedings are enrolled, whereas, in courts not of record, the proceedings are not enrolled. The privilege of having these enrolled memorials constitutes the great leading distinction between courts of record and courts not of record.

To be a court of record a court must have four characteristics, and may have a fifth, they are:

(1) *"A judicial tribunal having attributes and exercising functions independently of the person of the magistrate designated generally to hold it"* **[Jones v. Jones, 188 Mo.App. 220, 175 S.W. 227, 229; Ex parte Gladhill, 8 Metc. Mass.,**

171, per Shaw, C.J. See, also, Ledwith v. Rosalsky, 244 N.Y. 406, 155 N.E. 688, 689] [Black's Law Dictionary, 4th Ed., 425, 426] "Judges are magistrates" **[N.Y. CRC. LAW § 30 : NY Code - Section 30:]**

(2) *"Proceeding according to the course of common law"* **[Jones v. Jones, 188 Mo.App. 220, 175 S.W. 227, 229; Ex parte Gladhill, 8 Metc. Mass., 171, per Shaw, C.J. See, also, Ledwith v. Rosalsky, 244 N.Y. 406, 155 N.E. 688, 689] [Black's Law Dictionary, 4th Ed., 425, 426]**

(3) *"Its acts and judicial proceedings are enrolled, or recorded, for a perpetual memory and testimony."* **[3 Bl. Comm. 24; 3 Steph. Comm. 383; The Thomas Fletcher, C.C.Ga., 24 F. 481; Ex parte Thistleton, 52 Cal 225; Erwin v. U.S., D.C.Ga., 37 F. 488, 2 L.R.A. 229; Heininger v. Davis, 96 Ohio St. 205, 117 N.E. 229, 231]**

(4) *"Has power to fine or imprison for contempt."* **[3 Bl. Comm. 24; 3 Steph. Comm. 383; The Thomas Fletcher, C.C.Ga., 24 F. 481; Ex parte Thistleton, 52 Cal 225; Erwin v. U.S., D.C.Ga., 37 F. 488, 2 L.R.A. 229; Heininger v. Davis, 96 Ohio St. 205, 117 N.E. 229, 231] [Black's Law Dictionary, 4th Ed., 425, 426]**

(5) *"Generally possesses a seal."* **[3 Bl. Comm. 24; 3 Steph. Comm. 383; The Thomas Fletcher, C.C.Ga., 24 F. 481; Ex parte Thistleton, 52 Cal 225; Erwin v. U.S., D.C.Ga., 37 F. 488, 2 L.R.A. 229; Heininger v. Davis, 96 Ohio St. 205, 117 N.E. 229, 231] [Black's Law Dictionary, 4th Ed., 425, 426]**

The people of this State, as the successors of its former sovereign, are entitled to all the rights which formerly belonged to the King by his prerogative. **[Lansing v. Smith, 4 Wend. 9 (N.Y.) (1829), 21 Am. Dec. 89 10C Const. Law Sec. 298; 18 C Em.Dom. Sec. 3, 228; 37 C Nav.Wat. Sec. 219; Nuls Sec. 167; 48 C Wharves**

Sec. 3, 7] *"A consequence of this prerogative is the legal ubiquity of the king. His majesty in the eye of the law is always present in all his courts, though he cannot personally distribute justice".* **(Fortesc.c.8. 2Inst.186)** *"His judges are the mirror by which the king's image is reflected".* **[Blackstone's Commentaries, 270,]**

XIV. JUDICIAL IMMUNITY

New York judges are under the illusion that they have absolute immunity but all the cases that are sited making such a claim are without authority [people] and will fail in the federal and state courts in a court of record. Only the people are sovereign, all servants are under statutes and therefore liable to USC 18 and 42. *"Where there is no jurisdiction, there can be no discretion",* they are not above the law, when they commit a crime they will go to jail and are subject to civil suits. *"No man in this country is so high that he is above the law. No officer of the law may set that law at defiance with impunity. All the officers of the government, from the highest to the lowest, are creatures of the law and are bound to obey it."* ... *"It is the only supreme power in our system of government, and every man who, by accepting office participates in its functions, is only the more strongly bound to submit to that supremacy, and to observe the limitations which it imposes on the exercise of the authority which it gives."* **[U.S. v. Lee, 106 U.S. 196, 220 1 S. Ct. 240, 261, 27 L. Ed 171 (1882)]**

"There is a general rule that a ministerial officer who acts wrongfully, although in good faith, is nevertheless liable in a civil action and cannot claim the immunity of the sovereign". **[Cooper v. O'Conner, 99 F.2d 133]** *"Any judge who does not comply with his oath to the Constitution of the United States wars against that Constitution and engages in acts in violation of the supreme law of the land. The judge is engaged in acts of treason."* **[Cooper v. Aaron, 358 U.S. 1, 78 S. Ct. 1401 (1958)]** *"A judge must be acting within his jurisdiction as to subject matter and person, to be entitled to immunity from civil action*

for his acts." [**Davis v. Burris, 51 Ariz. 220, 75 P.2d 689 (1938)**]
"The courts are not bound by an officer's interpretation of the law under which he presumes to act." [**Hoffsomer v. Hayes, 92 Okla 32, 227 F. 417**] *"Where there is no jurisdiction, there can be no discretion, for discretion is incident to jurisdiction."* [**Piper v. Pearson, 2 Gray 120, cited in Bradley v. Fisher, 13 Wall. 335, 20 L.Ed. 646 (1872)**]

XVI. RIGHT TO PRACTICE LAW

"The term [liberty] ... denotes not merely freedom from bodily restraint but also the right of the individual to contract, to engage in any of the common occupations of life, to acquire useful knowledge, to marry, to establish a home and bring up children, to worship God according to the dictates of this own conscience... The established doctrine is that this liberty may not be interfered with, under the guise of protecting public interest, by legislative action." [**Meyer v. Nebraska, 262 U.S. 390, 399, 400**]

"A State cannot exclude a person from the practice of law or from any other occupation in a manner or for reasons that contravene the Due Process Clause of the Fourteenth Amendment". [**Schware v. Board of Bar Examiners, 353 U.S. 232 (1957)**]

"There can be no sanction or penalty imposed upon one because of his exercise of Constitutional Rights." [**Sherar v. Cullen, 481 F. 2d 946 (1973)**]

"The practice of law cannot be licensed by any state/State." [**Schware v. Board of Examiners, United State Reports 353 U.S. pages 238, 239**]

"The practice of law is an occupation of common right." [**Sims v. Aherns, 271 SW 720 (1925)**]

"The assertion of federal rights, when plainly and reasonably made, are not to be defeated under the name of local practice." **[Davis v. Wechler, 263 U.S. 22, 24; Stromberb v. California, 283 U.S. 359; NAACP v. Alabama, 375 U.S. 449]**

"... the right to file a lawsuit pro se is one of the most important rights under the constitution and laws." **[Elmore v. McCammon [(1986) 640 F. Supp. 905]**

XVII. RIGHT TO ASSIST

"Litigants can be assisted by unlicensed laymen during judicial proceedings." **[Brotherhood of Trainmen v. Virginia ex rel. Virginia State Bar, 377 U.S. 1; v. Wainwright, 372 U.S. 335; Argersinger v. Hamlin, Sheriff 407 U.S. 425]**

"A next friend is a person who represents someone who is unable to tend to his or her own interest." **[Federal Rules of Civil Procedures, Rule 17, 28 USCA "Next Friend]**

"Members of groups who are competent non-lawyers can assist other members of the group achieve the goals of the group in court without being charged with 'unauthorized practice of law'." **[NAACP v. Button, 371 U.S. 415); United Mineworkers of America v. Gibbs, 383 U.S. 715; and Johnson v. Avery, 89 S. Ct. 747 (1969)]**

"There, every man is independent of all laws, except those prescribed by nature. He is not bound by any institutions formed by his fellowman without his consent." **[Cruden v. Neale, 2 N.C. 338 (1796) 2 S.E.]**

"Under our system of government upon the individuality and intelligence of the citizen, the state does not claim to control him/her, except as his/her conduct to others, leaving him/her the sole judge as to all that affects himself/herself." **[Mugler v. Kansas 123 U.S. 623, 659-60.]**

"The assertion of federal rights, when plainly and reasonably made, is not to be defeated under the name of local practice." **[Davis v. Wechsler, 263 US 22, at 24]**

"A State may not impose a charge for the enjoyment of a right granted by the Federal Constitution." **[Murdock v. Pennsylvania, 319 U.S. 105, at 113]**

"The State cannot diminish rights of the people." **[Hertado v. California, 110 U.S. 516]** *"The Claim and exercise of a Constitutional Right cannot be converted into a crime."* **[Miller v. U.S. , 230 F 2d 486. 489]** *"If the state converts a liberty into a privilege the citizen can engage in the right with impunity"* **[Shuttlesworth v Birmingham , 373 USs 262]**

XVIII. HISTORY OF THE SHERIFF

While most people in America recognize the sheriff as the **Chief Law Enforcement Officer (CLEO)** for the county, they would be surprised to know that the office of sheriff has a proud history that spans well over a thousand years, from the early Middle Ages to our own "high-tech" era.

THE BEGINNING: THE MIDDLE AGES - More than 1,300 years ago in England, small groups of Anglo-Saxons lived in rural communities similar to modern day towns. Often at war, they decided to better organize themselves for defense. Sometime before the year 700, they formed a system of local self-government based on groups of ten. Each of the towns divided into groups of ten families, called tithing's. Each tithing elected a leader called a tithing man. The next level of government was a group of ten tithing's (or 100 families), and this group elected its own chief. The Anglo-Saxon word for chief was gerefa, later shortened to reeve. During the next two centuries, groups of hundreds banded together to form a new, higher unit of government called the shire. The shire was the forerunner of the modern county. Each shire had a chief (reeve) as well, and the more powerful official became known as a shire-reeve. The word shire-reeve became the modern English word sheriff - the chief of the county. The sheriff maintained law and order within his own county with the assistance of the citizens. When the sheriff sounded the 'hue and cry' that a criminal was at large, anyone who heard the alarm was responsible for bringing the criminal to justice. This principle of **citizen participation** survives today in the procedure known as **posse comitatus**.

THE OFFICE GROWS - English government eventually became more centralized under the power of a single ruler, the king. The king distributed huge tracts of land to noblemen, who governed the land under the King's authority. The office of sheriff was no longer elected but appointed by the noblemen for the counties they controlled. In those areas not consigned to noblemen, the king appointed his own sheriffs. After the Battle of Hastings in 1066, England's rule fell to the Normans (France) who seized and centralized all power under the Norman king and his appointees. The sheriff became the agent of the king, and among his new duties was tax collection. This dictatorial rule by a series of powerful kings became intolerable, and in 1215, an army of rebellious noblemen forced the despotic King John to sign the Magna Carta. This important document restored a number of rights to the noblemen and guaranteed certain basic freedoms. The text of the Magna Carta mentioned the important role of the sheriff nine times.

Over the next few centuries, the sheriff remained the leading law enforcement officer of the county. It was an honor to be appointed sheriff, but it was costly. If the people of the county did not pay the full amount of their taxes and fines, the sheriff was required to make up the difference out of his own pocket. He also had to provide lavish entertainment for judges and visiting dignitaries at his own expense.

THE SHERIFF CROSSES THE ATLANTIC - The first American counties were established in Virginia in 1634, and records show that one of these counties elected a sheriff in 1651. Most other colonial sheriffs were appointed. Just as the noblemen in medieval

England, large American landowners appointed sheriffs to enforce the law in the areas they controlled and to protect their lands. American sheriffs were not expected to pay extraordinary expenses, however, and some actually made money from the job.

Throughout the eighteenth and nineteenth centuries, colonial and state legislatures assigned a broad range of responsibilities to the sheriff which included the familiar role of law enforcement and tax collection. Other duties were new, such as overseeing jails, houses of corrections and work houses.

As Americans moved westward, so did the office of sheriff and the use of jails. Settlers desperately needed the sheriff to establish order in the lawless territories where power belonged to those with the fastest draw and the most accurate shot. Most western sheriffs, however, kept the peace by virtue of their authority. With a few exceptions, sheriffs resorted to firepower much less often than we have seen depicted in movies and on TV.

THE SHERIFF TODAY - There are over 3,000 counties in the United States, and almost every one of them has a sheriff, except for Alaska. Some cities, such as Denver, St. Louis, Richmond and Baltimore, have sheriffs as well. The office of sheriff is established either by the state constitution or by an act of state legislature. There are only two states in which the sheriff is not elected by the voters. In Rhode Island, sheriffs are appointed by the governor; in Hawaii, deputy sheriffs serve in the Department of Public Safety's Sheriff's Division.

There is really no such thing as a "typical" sheriff. Some sheriffs still have time to drop by the town coffee shop to chat with the citizens each day, while others report to an office in a skyscraper and manage a department whose budget exceeds that of many corporations. However, most sheriffs have certain roles and responsibilities in common.

Law Enforcement. A sheriff always has the power to make

arrests within his or her own county. Some states extend this authority to adjacent counties or to the entire state. Many sheriffs' offices also perform routine patrol functions such as traffic control, accident investigations, and transportation of prisoners. Larger departments may perform criminal investigations, and some unusually large sheriffs' offices command an air patrol, a mounted patrol, or a marine patrol.

Sheriffs still enlist the aid of the citizens. The National Neighborhood Watch Program, sponsored by the National Sheriffs' Association, allows citizens and law enforcement officials to cooperate in keeping communities safe. This is why the new mission of the Indiana Sheriff's Association and slogan is "Building Communities of Trust is ALL 92 Indiana Counties."

As the sheriff's law enforcement duties become more extensive and complex, new career opportunities exist for people with specialized skills: underwater diving, piloting, boating, skiing, radar technology, communications, computer technology, accounting, emergency medicine, and foreign languages (especially Spanish, French, and Vietnamese.)

Court Duties. Sheriffs are responsible for maintaining the safety and security of the court. A sheriff or deputy may be required to attend all court sessions; to act as bailiff; to take charge of juries whenever they are outside the courtroom; to serve court papers; to extradite prisoners; to collect taxes, or to perform other court-related functions.

Jail Administration. Most sheriffs' offices maintain and operate county jails or other detention centers, community corrections facilities such as work-release, and halfway houses. Sheriffs are responsible for supervising inmates, protecting their rights and providing food, clothing, exercise, recreation and medical services. As jail conditions continue to improve, sheriffs and their departments are earning increased respect and recognition as professionals.

Law enforcement is becoming increasingly complex. For the progressive, forward-looking sheriffs' offices of today, education and training are the keys to effective job performance. Today's sheriff is likely to have a college degree, a graduate degree in criminal justice, law or public administration, and several years' experience in the criminal justice system.

Your Indiana Sheriff's Association (ISA), under the leadership of Executive Director Stephen P. Luce, is dedicated to working with ISA membership to insure that the men and women who protect and serve the citizens of Indiana are the best trained and most qualified.

President Ronald Reagan stressed the importance of the modern sheriff in his address to the National Sheriffs' Association on June 21, 1984. He said, *"Thank you for standing up for this nation's dream of personal freedom under the rule of law. Thank you for standing against those who would transform that dream into a nightmare of wrongdoing and lawlessness. And thank you for your service to your communities, to your country, and to the cause of law and justice."*

Justice Scalia writing for the majority in a 1997 decision said that the "States are not subject to federal direction" and that the US Congress only had "discreet and enumerated powers" and that federal impotency was "rendered express" by the Tenth Amendment, he confirmed that **the Sheriff is the Chief Law Enforcement Officer (CLEO) of the county** and also proclaimed that the States "retain an inviolable sovereignty." Scalia went even further in this landmark decision, one in which two small-town sheriffs headed the Feds "off at the pass" and sent them on their way. Scalia, in his infinite obligation to the Constitution, took this entire ruling to the tenth power when he said, *"The Constitution protects us from our own best intentions... so that we may resist the temptation to concentrate power in one location as an expedient solution to the crisis of the day."* Obviously the Sheriff is the Peoples last line of defense against a government gone rogue.

XIX. FIRST PRINCIPAL

Liberty is mastered in three powers **(1) Light** (God) **(2) Justice** synonymous with virtue (Judicial process) **(3) Rule of destiny** (political process): Remove any one and you lose Liberty. America has lost its way and only a virtuous people can guide her back. And, so to that end the People by the mercy of God have rediscovered the common [natural] law grand jury and with His blessings shall return America to her roots again.

VIRTUE, maxims of law avow that justice and virtue are synonymous, before a man can implement justice he must first possess virtue which the Bible declares flows from the Lord alone (Luke 6:19) and defines virtue as whatsoever things are true, honest, just, pure, lovely, and of good report (Phil 4:8) the Lord further expounds saying the wisdom that is from above is first pure, then peaceable, gentle, and easy to be entreated, full of mercy and good fruits, without partiality, and without hypocrisy (James 3:17) and that he that follows after it establishes righteousness, and honor (Prov 21:21).

Thomas Jefferson understood this when he said: *"God who gave us life gave us liberty. And can the liberties of a nation be thought secure when we have removed their only firm basis, a conviction in the minds of the people that These liberties are of the gift of God? That they are not to be violated but with His wrath? Indeed, I tremble for my country when I reflect that God is just that His justice cannot sleep forever".*

George Washington understood this when he said: *"The favorable smiles of Heaven can never be expected on a nation that disregards The eternal rules of order and right which Heaven itself has ordained".*

Benjamin Franklin understood this when he said: *"Only a virtuous people are capable of freedom. As nations become corrupt and vicious, they have more need of masters".*

John Adams understood this when he said: *"Our Constitution was made only for a moral and religious people. It is wholly inadequate to the government of any other".*

Patrick Henry understood this when he said: *"It cannot be emphasized too strongly or too often that <u>this great nation was founded</u>, not by religionists, but by Christians; not on religions, but <u>on the Gospel of Jesus Christ</u>. For this very reason peoples of other faiths have been afforded asylum, prosperity, and freedom of worship here".*

James Madison understood this when he said: *"We have staked the whole future of American civilization, not upon the power of government, far from it. We have staked the future of all of our political institutions upon the capacity of mankind for self-government; upon the capacity of each and all of us to govern ourselves, to control ourselves, to sustain ourselves According to the Ten Commandments of God".*

Noah Webster understood this when he said: *"No truth is more evident to my mind than that the Christian religion must be the basis of any government intended to secure the rights and privileges of a free people".* **(Father of American Scholarship and Education)**

XX. THE NAME GAME — PEOPLE OR CITIZEN

14th Amendment Article I, section 1 - All persons born or naturalized in the United States, and subject to the jurisdiction thereof, are citizens of the United States and of the State wherein they reside. No State shall make or enforce any law which shall abridge the privileges or immunities of citizens of the United States; nor shall any State deprive any person of life, liberty, or property, without due process of law; nor deny to any person within its jurisdiction the equal protection of the laws.

NATION - in American constitutional law the word "state" is applied to the several members of the American Union, while the word "nation" is applied to the whole body of the people embraced within the jurisdiction of the federal government. **[Cooley, Const.Lim. 1; Texas v. White, 7 Wall. 720, 19 L. Ed. 227]**

PRIVILEGE - [Black's Law 4th edition, 1891] is merely an accessory of the debt which it secures, and falls with the extinguishment of the debt.

PERSONS - [Black's Law 4th edition, 1891] are divided by Law into natural and artificial. ... "corporations" or "bodies politic." Quasi municipal corporations - Bodies politic and corporate, created for the sole purpose of performing one or more municipal functions.

WE THE PEOPLE of the United States, in order to form a more perfect union, establish justice, insure domestic tranquility, provide for the common defense, promote the general welfare, and secure the blessings of liberty to ourselves and our posterity, do ordain and establish this Constitution for the United States of America.

PEOPLE - are supreme, not the state. **[Waring vs. the Mayor of Savanah]**; The state cannot diminish rights of the people. **[Hertado v. California]**; ...at the Revolution, the sovereignty devolved on the people; and they are truly the sovereigns of the country, but they are sovereigns without subjects...with none to govern but themselves. **[CHISHOLM v. GEORGIA]**: The people of this State, as the successors of its former sovereign, are entitled to all the rights which formerly belonged to the King by his prerogative. **[Lansing v. Smith]**

ORDAIN - to enact a constitution or law. **[State v. Dallas City]**

KING - is the sovereign, ruler, holds the highest executive power, a.k.a. the People; "Sovereignty itself is, of course, not subject to law, for it is the author and source of law; but in our system, while sovereign powers are delegated to the agencies of government, sovereignty itself remains with the people, by whom and for whom all government exists and acts And the law is the definition and limitation of power." **[Yick Wo v. Hopkins]**

XXI. NO GOD NO LIBERTY
- KNOW GOD KNOW LIBERTY

"If the Son therefore shall make you free, ye shall be free indeed." — **Jesus at John 8:36**

"If a nation expects to be both ignorant and free... it expects what never was and never will be." — **Thomas Jefferson**

"The favorable smiles of Heaven can never be expected on a nation that disregards The eternal rules of order and right which Heaven itself has ordained." — **George Washington**

"God who gave us life gave us liberty. And can the liberties of a nation be thought secure when we have removed their only firm basis, a conviction in the minds of the people that These liberties are of the gift of God? That they are not to be violated but with His wrath? Indeed, I tremble for my country when I reflect that God is just that His justice cannot sleep forever." — **Thomas Jefferson**

"The fate of unborn millions will now depend, under God, on the courage of this army, Our cruel and unrelenting enemy leaves us only the choice of brave resistance, or the most abject submission, We have, therefore to resolve to conquer or die." — **George Washington**

"I am sure that never was a people, who had more reason to acknowledge a Divine interposition in their affairs, than those of the United States; and I should be pained to believe that they have forgotten that agency, which was so often manifested during our Revolution, or That they failed to consider the omnipotence of that God who is alone able to protect them." — **George Washington**

"Only a virtuous people are capable of freedom. As nations become corrupt and vicious, they have more need of masters."
— **Benjamin Franklin**

"Our Constitution was made only for a moral and religious people. It is wholly inadequate to the government of any other."
— **John Adams**

"Statesmen, my dear Sir, may plan and speculate for liberty, but It is religion and morality alone, which can establish the principles upon which freedom can securely stand. The only foundation of a free constitution is pure virtue; and if this cannot be inspired into our people in a greater measure than they have it now, they may change their rulers and the forms of government, but they will not obtain a lasting liberty. They will only exchange tyrants and tyrannies." — **John Adams**

"The safety and prosperity of nations ultimately and Essentially depend on the protection and blessing of Almighty God; and the national acknowledgment of this truth is not only an indispensable duty, which the people owe to him, but a duty whose natural influence is favorable to the Promotion of that morality and piety, without which social happiness cannot exist, nor the blessings of a free government be enjoyed."
— **John Adams**

"Observe good faith and justice towards all Nations. Cultivate peace and harmony with all. Religion and Morality enjoin this conduct; and can it be that good policy does not equally enjoin it? Can it be that Providence has not connected the permanent felicity of a Nation with its virtue?"
— **George Washington**

"Nothing can contribute to true happiness that is inconsistent with duty; nor can a course of action conformable to it, be finally without an ample reward. For, God governs; and he is good." — **Benjamin Franklin**

"Happiness, whether in despotism or democracy, whether in slavery or liberty, can never be found without virtue."
— **John Adams**

"It cannot be emphasized too strongly or too often that this great nation was founded, not by religionists, but by Gods children; not on religions, but on the Gospel of Jesus Christ. For this very reason peoples of other faiths have been afforded asylum, prosperity, and freedom of worship here."
— **Patrick Henry**

"It is the duty of every man to render to the Creator such homage? Before any man can be considered as a member of Civil Society, he must be considered as a subject of the Governor of the Universe?" — **James Madison**

"We have staked the whole future of American civilization, not upon the power of government, far from it. We have staked the future of all of our political institutions upon the capacity of mankind for self-government; upon the capacity of each and all of us to govern ourselves, to control ourselves, to sustain ourselves According to the Ten Commandments of God."
— **James Madison**

"Religion, or the duty we owe to our Creator, and manner of discharging it, can be directed only by reason and conviction, not by force or violence." — **James Madison**

"Let it simply be asked where is the security for prosperity, for reputation, for life, if the sense of Religious obligation desert the oaths, which are The instruments of investigation in the Courts of Justice?" — **George Washington**

"And let us with caution indulge the supposition, that morality can be maintained without religion. Whatever may be conceded to the influence of refined education on minds of peculiar structure, reason and experience both Forbid us to expect that national morality can prevail in exclusion of religious

principle." — **George Washington**

" 'Tis substantially true, that Virtue or morality is a necessary spring of popular government." — **George Washington**

"Though, in reviewing the incidents of my Administration, I am unconscious of intentional error, I am nevertheless too sensible of my defects not to think it probable that I may have committed many errors. Whatever they may be I fervently beseech the Almighty to avert or mitigate the evils to which they may tend." — **George Washington**

Congress and President George Washington in 1789 passed the **United States Annotated Code, Article III** which states: *"Religion, morality, and knowledge, being necessary to good government and the happiness of mankind, schools and the means of education shall forever be encouraged."*

XXII. RELIGION IN LAW AND GOVERNMENT

"In my view, the Christian religion is the most important and one of the first things in which all children, under a free government ought to be instructed ? No truth is more evident to my mind than that the Christian religion must be the basis of any government intended to secure the rights and privileges of a free people. - The "Father of American Scholarship and Education." — **Noah Webster**

"The brief exposition of the Constitution of the United States, will unfold to young persons the principles of republican government; and it is the sincere desire of the writer that our citizens should early understand that The genuine source of correct republican principles is the Bible, particularly the New Testament of the Christian religion." — **Noah Webster**

"The religion which has introduced civil liberty is the religion of Christ and His apostles, which enjoins humility, piety, and benevolence; which acknowledges in every person a brother,

or a sister, and a citizen with equal rights. This is genuine Christianity, and to this we owe our free Constitutions of Government." — **Noah Webster**

"The moral principles and precepts contained in the Scriptures ought to form the basis of all of our civil constitutions and laws ? All the miseries and evils which men suffer from vice, crime, ambition, injustice, oppression, slavery and war, proceed from their despising or neglecting the precepts contained in the Bible." — **Noah Webster**

"When you become entitled to exercise the right of voting for public officers, let it be impressed on your mind that, The preservation of a republican God commands you to choose for rulers just men who will rule in the fear of God government depends on the faithful discharge of this duty;" — **Noah Webster**

"If the citizens neglect their duty and place unprincipled men in office, the government will soon be corrupted; laws will be made not for the public good so much as for the selfish or local purposes;" — **Noah Webster**

George Mason, father of our Bill of Rights, 1787: "*Every master of slaves is born a petty tyrant. They bring the judgment of heaven upon a country. As nations cannot be rewarded or punished in the next world, they must be in this. By an inevitable chain of causes and effects, Providence punishes national sins, by national calamities.*"

Common Law is our Heritage! Liberty is our inheritance! We the people have been lulled asleep, we have been robbed and persuaded to sell our birth right. **James 1:25** *"Whoso looketh into the perfect law of liberty, and continueth therein, he being not a forgetful hearer, but a doer of the work, this man shall be blessed in his deed."*

"My people are destroyed for lack of knowledge?" **Hosea 4:6.**

"Wisdom is the principal thing; therefore get wisdom: and with all thy getting get understanding." **Prov 4:7.**

So ordained and Sealed

We the people, by the mercy and grace of God ordained with certain unalienable rights, among them the right to form and exercise this **25 people Grand Jury** in the spirit of the Magna Carta and our founding fathers, and in obedience to God for this County on behalf of the people, having recorded our authority with the county Clerk and the State Supreme Court chief Clerk by which we act in order to establish justice, insure domestic tranquility, secure the blessings of liberty to ourselves and our posterity by the securing of Natural Law and thereby returning Justice, Honor, and Grace for a perpetual administration of trust on behalf of the people hereby defined in this handbook.

We the People

"ONLY THE PEOPLE" CAN SAVE AMERICA

WILL YOU? - THEN REGISTER WITH THE "NATIONAL REGISTRY"

At **www.NationalLibertyAlliance.org** to become a common law Jurist. We are establishing Common Law Grand Juries in all 3,141 counties in the United States of America. By doing this the people will move our Courts back to "Courts of Justice" and take 100% control of our government.

Watch the video **"Power of the Grand Jury." THE DUTY OF THE "COMMON LAW GRAND JURY"** is to right any wrong.

If anyone's unalienable rights have been violated, or removed, without a legal sentence of their peers, the Grand Jury can restore them.

In addition, if a dispute shall arise concerning this matter it shall be settled according to the judgment of the Grand Jurors, the Sureties of the peace.

IN A US SUPREME COURT STUNNING 6 TO 3 DECISION JUSTICE ANTONIN SCALIA, writing for the majority, confirmed that the American grand jury is neither part of the judicial, executive nor legislative branches of government, but instead belongs to the people. It is in effect a fourth branch of government "governed" and "administered" directly by and on behalf of the American people, and its authority emanates from the "Bill of Rights" and has the power to enforce law and remove people from PUBLIC office.

FREQUENTLY ASKED QUESTIONS:

Q: Once I register what happens next?
A: If you want to be an active full time or part time Grand Jurist notify one of your county coordinators and they will assist you, you can find them listed under county coordinator at **www.NationalLibertyAlliance.org** - Otherwise your name will go into the jury pool and you will receive a phone call occasionally to participate as a trial or grand jurist.

Q: Do I have to serve when I get the call?
A: No. If you cannot participate at that time, we will recycle your name, no questions asked.

Q: When I am called how long will I be needed for?
A: Usually 1-3 days, you will be given that information and the dates in order to decide if you can participate.

Q: What do I do now?
A: Go to **www.NationalLibertyAlliance.org** and Register. After you register you will be taken to an "Orientation Page" and you will be instructed further, please read carefully that page.

THE FIRST AMERICAN REVOLUTION

The First American Revolution did not start with "the shot heard round the world" on the morning of April 19, 1775. When British Regulars fired upon a small group of hastily assembled patriots on the Lexington Green, they were attempting to regain control of a colony they had already lost. The real Revolution, the transfer of political authority to the American patriots, occurred the previous summer when thousands upon thousands of farmers and artisans seized power from every Crown-appointed official in Massachusetts outside of Boston.

Starting in August 1774, each time a court was slated to meet under British authority in some Massachusetts town, great numbers of angry citizens made sure that it did not.

At Great Barrington, fifteen hundred patriots filled the courthouse to prevent the judges from entering. At Worcester, judges were made to read their recantations thirty times over, hats in hand, as they passed through 4,622 militiamen lined up along Main Street. So, too, at Springfield, where, "in a sandy, sultry place, exposed to the sun," once important officials sweated under the burden of their heavy black suits.

The functionaries of British rule cowered and collapsed, no match for the collective force of patriotic farmers. According to an eye-witness,

> The people of each town being drawn into separate companies marched with staves & musik. The trumpets sounding, drums beating, fifes playing and Colours flying, struck the passions of the soul into a proper tone, and inspired martial courage into each.[1]

The governor's councilors, once elected but now appointed directly by the Crown, were also forced to resign. Thomas Oliver, lieutenant-governor of Massachusetts and a councilor as well, ceded to a crowd of four thousand assembled around his home in Cambridge.

Timothy Paine of Worcester was visited by two thousand men who demanded his resignation. He told a committee he would comply, but his word would not suffice—the people wanted it in writing. Even that was not enough: the crowed demanded that he come out of his house while a representative read his resignation aloud. Again Paine complied, and again the people wanted more: he would have to read his resignation himself, with his hat off, several times as he passed through the ranks. Nothing else would do.[2]

Through it all, the revolutionaries engaged in a participatory democracy which far outreached the intentions of the so-called "Founding Fathers." They gathered under no special leaders. Their ad hoc representatives, such as the five men elected to talk with Timothy Paine, operated according to instructions approved by the assembled crowd and reported back immediately to the body as whole

Even the nighttime mobs (and there were many) maintained a democratic aspect. In Braintree, two hundred men gathered on a Sunday at around 8:00 P.M. to remove some gunpowder from the powder house and to make the local sheriff burn two warrants he was attempting to deliver. Successful in their missions, they wanted to celebrate with a loud "Huzzah." But should they disturb the Sabbath? "They called a vote," wrote Abigail Adams, who observed the affair, and "it being Sunday evening it passed in the negative."[3]

By early October 1774, more than six months before the red dawn at Lexington, all Crown-appointed officials had been forced to disavow British authority or flee to Boston, which was still under military protection. "The Flames of Sedition," wrote Governor Thomas Gage, had "spread universally throughout the Country beyond Conception."[4] The British had lost all control of the Massachusetts countryside, and they would never get it back.

Scholars differ widely on how to define "Revolution," but a good starting point, firmly-rooted in common usage, can be found in the Random House Webster' college Dictionary (1997): "a complete and forcible overthrow and replacement of an established government or political system by the people governed."

So in the late summer and early fall of 1774, the people of rural Massachusetts completely and forcibly overthrew the established government and began to set up their own; this was the first American Revolution. While a group of renowned lawyers, merchants, and slave-owning planters were meeting as a Continental Congress in Philadelphia to consider whether or not they should challenge British rule, the plain farmers and artisans of Massachusetts, guarding their liberties jealously and voting at every turn, wrested control from the most powerful empire on earth.

CONSTITUTION OF A
COMMON LAW GRAND JURY
Lex Naturalis Dei Gratia

We the people of the United States of America do pledge to the Governor of the Universe, in our capacity as Jurist, both Grand and Trial, to uphold the US Constitution, to carry out the principles of natural law in all of our judgments; in order to establish justice, insure domestic tranquility, secure the blessings of liberty to ourselves and our posterity by deliberating under Natural Law, principled under Justice, Honor, and Mercy for a perpetual administration of trust on behalf of the people, acknowledging the foundation upon which all Law weighs, Charity. Inasmuch as for the sake of God, for the bettering of our sovereignty, if any of our civil servants shall have transgressed against any of the people in any respect (and they shall ask us to cause that error to be amended without delay) or shall have broken some one of the articles of peace or security, <u>and their transgression shall have been shown to four   Jurors of the aforesaid twenty-five</u> and if those four Jurors are unable to settle the transgression, they shall come to the twenty-five, showing to the Grand Jury the error which shall be enforced by the law of the land.

It is the Duty of the Grand Jury, if anyone's unalienable rights have been violated, or removed, without a legal sentence of their peers, from their lands, home, liberties or lawful right, we [the twenty-five] shall straightway restore them. And if a dispute shall arise concerning this matter it shall be settled according to the judgment of the twenty-five Grand Jurors, the sureties of the peace.

A legal maxim - every right when withheld must have a remedy, and every injury it's proper redress.[5] — William Blackstone[6]

There is a common Law principle which states that for their to be a crime, there must first be a victim, *corpus delicti*. In the absence of a victim there can be no crime. The State cannot be the victim.

Statutes are not law[7], servant legislators cannot write statutes[8] to control the behavior of their masters.

FOOTNOTES

[1] **James R. Trumbull**, *History of Northampton, Massachusetts, from its Settlement in 1654* (Northampton: Press of Gazette Printing Co., 1902), 348.

[2] **For** Oliver's resignation, see chapter 4, note 72; for Paine's resignation, see chapter 3, notes 39-46.

[3] **Abigail to John Adams,** September 14, 1774, L.H. Butterfield, ed., *Adams Family Correspondence* (Cambridge: Belknap Press, 1963), 1: 152.

[4] **Gage to Lord Dartmouth,** September 2, 1774, Clarence E. Carter, ed., *Correspondence of General Thomas Gage* (New Haven: Yale University Press, 1931), 1: 370.

— — —

[5] **Marbury v. Madison, 5 u.s. 137 (1803)** *"...the government of the United States has been emphatically termed <u>a government of laws, and not of men</u>. It will certainly cease to deserve this high appellation if the laws furnish no remedy for the violation of a vested legal right."*

[6] **Hoke v. Henderson, 15 u.s. 15,25 am. dec. 677.** *"...that statutes which would deprive a citizen of the rights of person or property without a regular trial, according to the course and usage of common law, would not be the law of the land."*

[7] **Rodriques v. Ray Donavan (U.S. Department of Labor) 769 F. 2s 1344, 1348 (1985).** *"All codes, rules, and regulations are for government authorities only, not human/creators in accordance with God's laws. All codes, rules, and regulations are unconstitutional and lacking due process..."*

[8] **Sherar v. Cullen, 481 F. 945** *"For a crime to exist, there must be an injured party. There can be no sanction or penalty imposed upon one because of his exercise of Constitutional right."*

THE UNITED STATES EXISTS IN TWO FORMS

The United States exists in two forms: The *original united States* which controlled the federal government until 1860; and the *federal United States* which was incorporated in 1871.

The government of the *original united States of America* was usurped by the government of the *federal United States* which only controls the *District of Columbia and its territories* (Washington, D.C.) as a for-profit corporation that acts as our National Government. The *Corporate United States* operates under public *commercial law* rather than private *common law*.

The original Constitution and the Declaration of Independence refer to *"these united States"*. The word *"united"* is an adjective describing the noun, *"States"*. Therefore the lower case *"united"*.

When the *federal United States* was formed in 1871 the adjective *"united"* was changed to the noun *"United"* because the *federal United States* is a corporation which word is not an adjective but a noun.

The Constitution of the *original united States of America* was never removed; it has lain dormant since 1871 and is still intact to this day. This point was made clear by Supreme Court Justice Marshall Harlan in *Downes v. Bidwell* 182, U.S. 244 1901 by the following dissenting opinion: *"Two national governments exist; one to be maintained under the Constitution with all its restrictions; the other to be maintained by Congress outside and independently of that Instrument."*

The *rewritten* 1871 *Constitution of the United States* (*Inc.*) overrides the *original Constitution for the united States of America,* which explains why our Congressmen and Senators don't abide by it and the President (CEO) of the Corporate United States can write Executive Orders to do whatever he wants to do. He is following corporate laws that completely *strip* sovereigns of their God given unalienable rights.

Corporate public *commercial law* is not sovereign (private), for it is a public agreement between two or more parties under public contract.

Common law (under which sovereigns operate) is not *commercial law*; common law is personal and private.

Source: Black's Law Dictionary, Sixth Edition (With Pronunciations)

Government *De facto*. A government of fact exercising power and control in the place of true and lawful government; a government not established according to the constitution of the nation, not lawfully entitled to recognition or supremacy but which has nevertheless supplanted or displaced the government *de jure*. A government deemed unlawful or wrongful and unjust, which, nevertheless, receives habitual obedience from the bulk of the commune (community).

There are several degrees of what is called *"de facto government"*. Such a government in its *highest* degree assumes a character closely resembling that of a lawful government. This is when the usurping government expels the regular authorities from their customary seats and functions and establishes itself in their place and becomes the actual government of a country.

The distinguishing characteristic of such a government is that its adherents, who are warring against the government *de jure,* do not incur the penalties of treason; and under certain limitations the obligations assumed by them in behalf of the country, or otherwise, will generally be respected by the *de jure* government when restored. Such a government might more aptly be denominated a *"government of paramount force"* maintained by military power against the rightful authority of an established and lawful government; and obeyed in civil matters by private citizens.

They are usually administered by military authority, but they may also be administered by civil authority supported more or less by military force.

Source: *Thorington v. Smith*, 75 U.S. (8 Wall.) 1, 19 L.Ed. 361.

***De facto* Government** - A government that maintains itself by a display of force against the will of the legal government, and is successful at least temporarily in overturning the institutions of the rightful government by setting up its own government in lieu thereof, *Wortham v.Walker,* 133 Tex. 255, 128 S.W.2d. 1138, 1145.

Government *De jure*. A government of right; a true and lawful government; a government established according to the constitution of the nation or state and lawfully entitled to recognition and the administration of the nation although actually cut off from power or control. A government deemed lawful, rightful and just, which has been nevertheless supplanted or displaced, which receives not habitual obedience from the bulk of the community.

De jure - A condition in which there has been total compliance with all requirements of law; of right; legitimate; lawful; by right and just title. In this sense it is the contrary of *de facto*. It may also be contrasted with *degratia,* in which case it means *"as a matter of right",* as *degratia* means *"by grace or favor".* Again, it may be contrasted with *deaequitate;* here meaning *"by law",* as the latter means *"by equity".*

Source; IBID: Black's Law Dictionary, Sixth Edition (With Pronunciations)

HOW THE CONSTITUTION WAS USURPED BY THE CORPORATION

The CORPORATE UNITED STATES is not obligated nor accountable to the People except to make a profit for its stockholders as a corporation. The corporate interest does not benefit the people but uses the people and their labor to make a profit for the corporation. This corporation works in concert with the corporate courts and banks to usurp the people's wealth. The transfer of the constitutional authority of the money over to a private foreign bank (the non-federal Federal Reserve) has devastated our lives. This crime of taking the money authority away from the People must be corrected and authority restored to a constitutional form of government so our country can become prosperous once again.

From a speech in Congress in Congressional Record of March 17, 1993, Vol. 33, page H-1303, regarding The Bankruptcy of the United States, by Speaker, Representative James Trafficant Jr. (Ohio), addressing the House:

"It is an established fact that the United States Federal Government has been dissolved by the Emergency Banking Act, March 9, 1933, 48 Stat. 1, Public Law 89-719; declared by President Roosevelt, being bankrupt and insolvent.

"H.J.R. 192, 73rd Congress in session June 5, 1933 – Joint Resolution To Suspend The Gold Standard and Abrogate The Gold Clause dissolved the Sovereign Authority of the United States and the official capacities of all United States Governmental Offices, Officers, and Departments and is further evidence that the United States Federal Government exists today in name only.

"The receivers of the United States Bankruptcy are the International Bankers, via the United Nations, the World Bank and the International Monetary Fund. All United States Offices, Officials, and Departments are now operating within a *de facto status* in name only under Emergency War Powers. With the Constitutional Republican form of Government now dissolved, the receivers of the Bankruptcy have adopted a new form of government for the United States. This new form of government is known as a Democracy, being an established Socialist/Communist order under a new governor for America. This act was instituted and established by transferring and/or placing the Office of the Secretary of Treasury to that of the Governor of the International Monetary Fund. Public Law 94-564, page 8, Section H.R. 13955 reads in part: "The U.S. Secretary of Treasury receives no compensation for representing the United States.

"Prior to 1913, most Americans owned clear, allodial title to property, free and clear of any liens of mortgages until the Federal Reserve Act (1913) "Hypothecated" all property within the Federal United States to the Board of Governors of the Federal Reserve, in which the Trustees (stockholders) held legal title. The U.S. Citizen (tenant, franchisee) was

49

registered as a "beneficiary" of the trust via his/her birth certificate. <u>In 1933, the Federal United States hypothecated all of the present and future properties, assets, and labor of their "subjects," the 14th Amendment U.S. Citizen to the Federal Reserve System</u>. In return, the Federal Reserve System agreed to extend the federal United States Corporation all of the credit "money substitute" it needed.

"Like any debtor, the Federal United States government had to assign collateral and security to their creditors as a condition of the loan. Since the Federal United States didn't have any assets, <u>they assigned the private property of their "economic slaves," the U.S. Citizens, as collateral against the federal debt</u>. They also pledged the unincorporated federal territories, national parks, forests, birth certificates, and non-profit organizations as collateral against the federal debt. <u>All has already been transferred as payment to the international bankers</u>.

"Unwittingly, America has returned to its pre-American Revolution feudal roots whereby all land is held by a sovereign and the common people have no rights to hold allodial title to property. Once again, <u>We the People are tenants and share-croppers renting our own property from a Sovereign in the guise of the Federal Reserve Bank</u>. We the People have exchanged one master for another."

HOW CAN WE REPAIR OUR COUNTRY RIGHT NOW?

As the Republic for the United States works to re-install its government, the knowledge and truth about what has happened needs to be told. All Americans need to know the history of this tragedy, but with the good news about how it all can be brought back. Much help is needed to correct all of the unconstitutional laws, codes, and programs that plague our country today. The Republic for the United States of America is not a movement, it is the lawful government of the United States. Become part of the re-establishment process; get involved with a Common Law Grand Jury and help to restore the Republic for the United States of America.

BILL OF RIGHTS

THE FIRST 10 AMENDMENTS
TO THE CONSTITUTION
AS RATIFIED BY THE STATES

Note: **The following text is a transcription of the first 10 amendments to the Constitution in their original form.** These amendments were ratified December 15, 1791, and form what is commonly known as the "Bill of Rights."

THE PREAMBLE TO THE BILL OF RIGHTS

Congress of the United States begun and held at the City of New-York, on Wednesday the fourth of March, one thousand seven hundred and eighty nine.

THE Conventions of a number of the States, having at the time of their adopting the Constitution, expressed a desire, in order to prevent misconstruction or abuse of its powers, that further declaratory and restrictive clauses should be added: And as extending the ground of public confidence in the Government, will best ensure the beneficent ends of its institution.

RESOLVED by the Senate and House of Representatives of the United States of America, in Congress assembled, two thirds of both Houses concurring, that the following Articles be proposed to the Legislatures of the several States, as amendments to the Constitution of the United States, all, or any of which Articles, when ratified by three fourths of the said Legislatures, to be valid to all intents and purposes, as part of the said Constitution; viz.

ARTICLES in addition to, and Amendment of the Constitution for the United States of America, proposed by Congress, and ratified by the Legislatures of the several States, pursuant to the fifth Article of the original Constitution.

AMENDMENT I

Congress shall make no law respecting an establishment of religion, or prohibiting the free exercise thereof; or abridging the freedom of speech, or of the press; or the right of the people peaceably to assemble, and to petition the Government for a redress of grievances.

AMENDMENT II

A well regulated Militia, being necessary to the security of a free State, the right of the people to keep and bear Arms, shall not be infringed.

AMENDMENT III

No Soldier shall, in time of peace be quartered in any house, without the consent of the Owner, nor in time of war, but in a manner to be prescribed by law.

AMENDMENT IV

The right of the people to be secure in their persons, houses, papers, and effects, against unreasonable searches and seizures, shall not be violated, and no Warrants shall issue, but upon probable cause, supported by Oath or affirmation, and particularly describing the place to be searched, and the persons or things to be seized.

AMENDMENT V

No person shall be held to answer for a capital, or otherwise infamous crime, unless on a presentment or indictment of a Grand Jury, except in cases arising in the land or naval forces, or in the Militia, when in actual service in time of War or public danger; nor shall any person be subject for the same offence to be twice put in jeopardy of life or limb; nor shall be compelled in any criminal case to be a witness against himself, nor be deprived of life, liberty, or property, without due process of law; nor shall private property be taken for public use, without just compensation.

AMENDMENT VI

In all criminal prosecutions, the accused shall enjoy the right to a speedy and public trial, by an impartial jury of the State and district wherein the crime shall have been committed, which district shall have been previously ascertained by law, and to be informed of the nature and cause of the accusation; to be confronted with the witnesses against him; to have compulsory process for obtaining witnesses in his favor, and to have the Assistance of Counsel for his defence.

AMENDMENT VII

In suits at common law, where the value in controversy shall   exceed twenty dollars, the right of trial by jury shall be preserved, and no fact tried by a jury, shall be otherwise reexamined in any Court of the United States, than according to the rules of the common law.

AMENDMENT VIII

Excessive bail shall not be required, nor excessive fines imposed, nor cruel and unusual punishments inflicted.

AMENDMENT IX

The enumeration in the Constitution, of certain rights, shall not be construed to deny or disparage others retained by the people.

AMENDMENT X

The powers not delegated to the United States by the Constitution, nor prohibited by it to the States, are reserved to the states respect-fully, or to the people.

Chain of Authority

God - Natural Law

|

We the People

|

Magna Carta – Declaration of Independence - Constitution

|

Legislature - Judicial - Administration

|

United States Citizens

DECLARATION OF INDEPENDENCE

IN CONGRESS, July 4, 1776.

The unanimous Declaration of the thirteen united States of America. When in the Course of human events, it becomes necessary for one people to dissolve the political bands which have connected them with another, and to assume among the powers of the earth, the separate and equal station to which the Laws of Nature and of Nature's God entitle them, a decent respect to the opinions of mankind requires that they should declare the causes which impel them to the separation.

We hold these truths to be self-evident, that all men are created equal, that they are endowed by their Creator with certain unalienable Rights, that among these are Life, Liberty and the pursuit of Happiness.--That to secure these rights, Governments are instituted among Men, deriving their just powers from the consent of the governed, --That whenever any Form of Government becomes destructive of these ends, it is the Right of the People to alter or to abolish it, and to institute new Government, laying its foundation on such principles and organizing its powers in such form, as to them shall seem most likely to effect their Safety and Happiness. Prudence, indeed, will dictate that Governments long established should not be changed for light and transient causes; and accordingly all experience hath shewn, that mankind are more disposed to suffer, while evils are sufferable, than to right themselves by abolishing the forms to which they are accustomed. But when a long train of abuses and usurpations, pursuing invariably the same Object evinces a design to reduce them under absolute Despotism, it is their right, it is their duty, to throw off such Government, and to provide new Guards for their future security.--Such has been the patient sufferance of these Colonies; and such is now the necessity which constrains them to alter their former Systems of Government. The history of the present King of Great Britain is a history of repeated injuries and usurpations, all having in direct object the establishment of an absolute Tyranny over these States.

To prove this, let Facts be submitted to a candid world.

He has refused his Assent to Laws, the most wholesome and necessary for the public good.

He has forbidden his Governors to pass Laws of immediate and pressing importance, unless suspended in their operation till his Assent should be obtained; and when so suspended, he has utterly neglected to attend to them.

He has refused to pass other Laws for the accommodation of large districts of people, unless those people would relinquish the right of Representation in the Legislature, a right inestimable to them and formidable to tyrants only.

He has called together legislative bodies at places unusual, uncomfortable, and distant from the depository of their public Records, for the sole purpose of fatiguing them into compliance with his measures.

He has dissolved Representative Houses repeatedly, for opposing with manly firmness his invasions on the rights of the people.

He has refused for a long time, after such dissolutions, to cause others to be elected; whereby the Legislative powers, incapable of Annihilation, have returned to the People at large for their exercise; the State remaining in the mean time exposed to all the dangers of invasion from without, and convulsions within.

He has endeavoured to prevent the population of these States; for that purpose obstructing the Laws for Naturalization of Foreigners; refusing to pass others to encourage their migrations hither, and raising the conditions of new Appropriations of Lands.

He has obstructed the Administration of Justice, by refusing his Assent to Laws for establishing Judiciary powers.

He has made Judges dependent on his Will alone, for the tenure of their offices, and the amount and payment of their salaries.

He has erected a multitude of New Offices, and sent hither swarms of Officers to harass our people, and eat out their substance. He has kept among us, in times of peace, Standing Armies without the Consent of our legislatures.

He has affected to render the Military independent of and superior to the Civil power.

He has combined with others to subject us to a jurisdiction foreign to our constitution, and unacknowledged by our laws; giving his Assent to their Acts of pretended Legislation:

For Quartering large bodies of armed troops among us:

For protecting them, by a mock Trial, from punishment for any Murders which they should commit on the Inhabitants of these States:

For cutting off our Trade with all parts of the world:

For imposing Taxes on us without our Consent:

For depriving us in many cases, of the benefits of Trial by Jury:

For transporting us beyond Seas to be tried for pretended offences

For abolishing the free System of English Laws in a neighbouring Province, establishing therein an Arbitrary government, and enlarging its Boundaries so as to render it at once an example and fit instrument for introducing the same absolute rule into these Colonies:

For taking away our Charters, abolishing our most valuable Laws, and altering fundamentally the Forms of our Governments:

For suspending our own Legislatures, and declaring themselves invested with power to legislate for us in all cases whatsoever.

He has abdicated Government here, by declaring us out of his Protection and waging War against us.

He has plundered our seas, ravaged our Coasts, burnt our towns, and destroyed the lives of our people.

He is at this time transporting large Armies of foreign Mercenaries to compleat (complete) the works of death, desolation and tyranny, already begun with circumstances of Cruelty & perfidy scarcely paralleled in the most barbarous ages, and totally unworthy the Head of a civilized nation.

He has constrained our fellow Citizens taken Captive on the high Seas to bear Arms against their Country, to become the executioners of their friends and Brethren, or to fall themselves by their Hands.

He has excited domestic insurrections amongst us, and has endeavoured to bring on the inhabitants of our frontiers, the merciless Indian Savages, whose known rule of warfare, is an undistinguished destruction of all ages, sexes and conditions.

In every stage of these Oppressions We have Petitioned for Redress in the most humble terms: Our repeated Petitions have been answered only by repeated injury. A Prince whose character is thus marked by every act which may define a Tyrant, is unfit to be the ruler of a free people.

Nor have We been wanting in attentions to our British brethren. We have warned them from time to time of attempts by their legislature to extend an unwarrantable jurisdiction over us. We have reminded them of the circumstances of our emigration and settlement here. We have appealed to their native justice and magnanimity, and we have conjured them by the ties of our common kindred to disavow these usurpations, which, would inevitably interrupt our connections and correspondence. They too have been deaf to the voice of justice and of consanguinity. We must, therefore, acquiesce in the necessity, which denounces our Separation, and hold them, as we hold the rest of mankind, Enemies in War, in Peace Friends.

We, therefore, the Representatives of the united States of America, in General Congress, Assembled, appealing to the Supreme Judge of the world for the rectitude of our intentions, do, in the Name, and by Authority of the good People of these Colonies, solemnly publish and declare, That these United Colonies are, and of Right ought to be Free and Independent States; that they are Absolved from all Allegiance to the British Crown, and that all political connection between them and the State of Great Britain, is and ought to be totally dissolved; and that as Free and Independent States, they have full Power to levy War, conclude Peace, contract Alliances, establish Commerce, and to do all other Acts and Things which Independent States may of right do. And for the support of this Declaration, with a firm reliance on the protection of divine Providence, we mutually pledge to each other our Lives, our Fortunes and our sacred Honor.

The 56 signatures on the Declaration appear in the positions indicated:

Georgia: Button Gwinnett, Lyman Hall, George Walton

North Carolina: William Hooper, Joseph Hewes, John Penn

South Carolina: Edward Rutledge, Thomas Heyward, Jr., Thomas Lynch, Jr., Arthur Middleton

Massachusetts: John Hancock

Maryland: Samuel Chase, William Paca, Thomas Stone, Charles Carroll of Carrollton

Virginia: George Wythe, Richard Henry Lee, Thomas Jefferson, Benjamin Harrison, Thomas Nelson, Jr., Francis Lightfoot Lee, Carter Braxton

Pennsylvania: Robert Morris, Benjamin Rush, Benjamin Franklin, John Morton, George Clymer, James Smith, George Taylor, James Wilson, George Ross

Delaware: Caesar Rodney, George Read, Thomas McKean

New York: William Floyd, Philip Livingston, Francis Lewis, Lewis Morris

New Jersey: Richard Stockton, John Witherspoon, Francis Hopkinson, John Hart, Abraham Clark

New Hampshire: Josiah Bartlett, William Whipple

Massachusetts: Samuel Adams, John Adams, Robert Treat Paine, Elbridge Gerry

Rhode Island: Stephen Hopkins, William Ellery

Connecticut: Roger Sherman, Samuel Huntington, William Williams, Oliver Wolcott

New Hampshire: Matthew Thornton

COMMON LAW GRAND JURY GROUND SWELL

HAVE you ever heard of a Common Law Grand Jury?

The Common Law Grand Jury is alive and well in over 26 States! There are 3141 counties in the United States of America and our goal is to get at least 6 people in each county in order to organize and election in your county to reinstate and initiate the common Law Grand Jury...Nation-wide!

When we reinstate the common Law Grand Jury in all the counties of a state then the people will have 100% control of their state government. When 26+ states achieve this goal We the People will then have 100% control of Washington, D.C.

DUTY OF THE "COMMON LAW" GRAND JURY

If anyone's unalienable rights have been violated, or removed, without a legal sentence of their peers, from their lands, home, liberties or lawful right, we [the twenty-five] shall straightway restore them. And if a dispute shall arise concerning this matter it shall be settled according to the judgment of the twenty-five Grand Jurors, the sureties of the peace. [MAGNA CARTA, JUNE 15, 1215, 52.]

It is the duty or the People to govern themselves and to secure their government by participating as a Jurist!

THINK ABOUT THIS

If we the people can reinstate justice and demand that elected officials and bureaucrats obey the law or be indicted, we would have then succeeded in reinstating the Constitution!

Only the People can stand up and defend the Constitution because the Constitution cannot defend itself, and bureaucrats will never do it.

In a stunning 6 to 3 decision Justice Antonin Scalia, writing for the majority [of supreme court Justices], confirmed that the American grand jury is neither part of the judicial, executive nor legislative branches of government, but instead belongs to the people. It is in effect a fourth branch of government "governed" and administered to directly by and on behalf of the American people, and its authority emanates from the Bill of Rights, see *United States v. Williams*.

"Hold on to the Constitution and the Republic for which it stands. Miracles do not cluster, and what has happened once in 6,000 years, may not happen again. Hold on to the constitution, for if the American constitution should fail, there will be anarchy throughout the world." — Daniel Webster.

"Necessity is the plea for every infringement of human freedom. It is the argument of tyrants; it is the creed of slaves." — William Pitt, Nov. 18, 1783.

"I would rather be exposed to the inconvenience attending too much Liberty than those attending too small degree of it." — Thomas Jefferson.

MISSION STATEMENT

Our Mission is to restore the people to sovereignty through knowledge, and only then will they be armed with the virtue to take political and judicial power. The people have it in their power to disarm and defeat the enemy of Liberty both foreign and domestic if they only understood the principles of freedom and stand upon them.

To take political power is to control our elected representatives, by bringing them into obedience through fear of the people, this is accomplished by understanding the office of and becoming an elected committeeman, and then executing the powers, it's that simple!

To take judicial power is to control our courts by understanding jurisdiction and bringing into subjection all government officers and officials using common law courts by opening courts of record and executing "people" authority, it's that simple!

But to successfully apply political and judicial power you must have a sense of justice and mercy which is synonymous with virtue, and to get virtue you need to have a relationship with your creator. If everyone exercised these principles America could shake off the chains or tyranny, reinstate out republic, and bring down the NWO "literally overnight". This is the only way to save the nation, without power you are powerless!

Join our endeavor and save our Republic, one people at a time!

We are Non Partisan - A partisan person is "one who is blindly or unreasonably devoted to party positions". Therefore a partisan cannot possibly serve the Constitution. George Washington warned us against political parties. He said *"they only succeed in pitting one group against another"*.

The cause of the grassroots movement is the awakening to our constitutional crisis, for grassroots engaged in partisan politics further serves the demise of our constitutional republic. The evil genius of the progressive movement is their exploitation of partizan politics, which they created, to subvert our Constitution.

Grassroots groups are natural and spontaneous, whose primary objective is to reinstate the Constitution; to be partisan would be counter productive.

The traditional power structures are orchestrated and designed to harness grassroots movements. "They must always be suspect" and will be proven corrupt, if they are partisan - divisive - and take control of choosing candidates.

Grassroots are founded locally; control is local and most events are local. To collaborate with distant groups is necessary for unity, but if events become dictated by them, you are not longer grassroots.

"All that is necessary for the triumph of evil is that good men do nothing." — **Edmund Burke.**

"The question before the people is one of an awful moment to the country. For my own part, I consider it as nothing less than a question of freedom or slavery; ... Should I keep back my opinions at such a time, through fear... it is natural to man to indulge in the illusions of hope, we are apt to shut

our eyes against a painful truth, and listen to the song of that siren till she transforms us into beasts. Is this the part of wise men, engaged in a great and arduous struggle for liberty? ... I have but one lamp by which my feet are guided; and that is the lamp of experience. I know no way of judging of the future, but by the past.

"They are sent over to bind and rivet upon us those chains which the ministry have been so long forging. And what have we to oppose to them? Shall we try argument? Sir, we have been trying that for the last ten years. Have we anything new to offer upon the subject? Nothing.

"Sir, we have done everything that could be done, to avert the storm which is now coming on. We have petitioned; we have remonstrated; we have supplicated; we have prostrated ourselves, and have employed its interposition to arrest the tyrannical hands of the ministry. Our petitions have been slighted; our remonstrances have produced additional violence and insult; our supplications have been disregarded; and we have been spurned, with contempt, from the foot of the throne. In vain, after these things, may we indulge the fond hope of peace and reconciliation. There is no longer any room for hope.

"If we wish to be free; if we mean to preserve privileges, if we mean not to abandon the noble struggle in which we have been so long engaged, and which we have pledged ourselves never to abandon until the glorious object of our contest shall be obtained, we must fight! I repeat it, sir, we must fight! An appeal to arms and to the God of Hosts is all that is left us!

"They tell us, Sir that we are weak; unable to cope with so formidable an adversary. But when shall we be stronger? Will it be the next week, or the next year? Will it be when we are totally disarmed, and when a guard shall be stationed in every house? Shall we gather strength by irresolution and inaction? Shall we acquire the means of effectual resistance, by lying supinely on our backs, and hugging the delusive phantom of hope, until our enemies shall have bound us hand and foot?

"Sir, we are not weak if we make a proper use of those means which the God of nature hath placed in our powers.

"Three [hundred] millions of people armed in the holy cause of liberty, and in such a country as that which we possess, are invincible by any force which our enemy can send against us.

"Besides, sir, we shall not fight our battles alone. There is a just God who presides over the destinies of nations; and who will raise up friends to fight our battles for us, it is now too late to retire from the contest. There is no retreat but in submission and slavery! Our chains are forged! Their clanking may be heard! The war is inevitable and let it come! I repeat it, sir, let it come.

"Gentlemen may cry Peace Peace, but there is no peace. The war has actually begun! The next fate that sweeps from the north will bring to our ears the clash of resounding arms! Our brethren are already in the field! Why stand we here idle? What is it that gentlemen wish? What should they have?

"Is life so dear, or peace so sweet, as to be purchased at the price of chains and slavery? Forbid it, Almighty God! I know not what course others may take; but as for me, give me liberty or give me death!" — **Patrick Henry**

See the web page;

NationalLibertyAlliance.org

If you have any questions or comments feel free to email:

David Robinson
drobin88@comcast.net

Administrator
*Unified Maine Common Law Grand Jury
for the Maine Republic Free State*

Thanks for standing up to save our Republic.

Made in the USA
Las Vegas, NV
26 February 2022

44626070R00036